THIS BOOK BELONGS TO

NAME	
Email	
Websites	

Signature Planner Journals

INDEX

PAGE	BIRD
1	
3	
5	
7	
9	
11	
13	
15	
17	
19	
21	
23	
25	
27	
29	
31	
33	
35	
37	
39	
41	
43	
45	
47	
49	

PAGE	BIRD
51	
53	
55	
57	
59	
61	
63	
65	
67	
69	
71	
73	
75	
77	
79	
81	
83	
85	
87	
89	
91	
93	
95	
97	
99	

BIRD WATCHING

DATE		TIME	
LOCATION			
WEATHER		**WIND**	
BIRD NAME			
SCIENTIFIC NAME			
FEATURES/ DESCRIPTION			
BIRDS ACTIONS			
MY ACTIONS			
HABITAT			

 ADDITIONAL NOTES

BIRD WATCHING

DATE		TIME	
LOCATION			
WEATHER		**WIND**	
BIRD NAME			
SCIENTIFIC NAME			
FEATURES/ DESCRIPTION			
BIRDS ACTIONS			
MY ACTIONS			
HABITAT			

ADDITIONAL NOTES

BIRD WATCHING

DATE		TIME	
LOCATION			
WEATHER		WIND	
BIRD NAME			
SCIENTIFIC NAME			
FEATURES/ DESCRIPTION			
BIRDS ACTIONS			
MY ACTIONS			
HABITAT			

ADDITIONAL NOTES

BIRD WATCHING

DATE		TIME	
LOCATION			
WEATHER		**WIND**	
BIRD NAME			
SCIENTIFIC NAME			
FEATURES/ DESCRIPTION			
BIRDS ACTIONS			
MY ACTIONS			
HABITAT			

ADDITIONAL NOTES

BIRD WATCHING

DATE		TIME	
LOCATION			
WEATHER		**WIND**	
BIRD NAME			
SCIENTIFIC NAME			
FEATURES/ DESCRIPTION			
BIRDS ACTIONS			
MY ACTIONS			
HABITAT			

ADDITIONAL NOTES

BIRD WATCHING

DATE		TIME	
LOCATION			
WEATHER		**WIND**	
BIRD NAME			
SCIENTIFIC NAME			
FEATURES/ DESCRIPTION			
BIRDS ACTIONS			
MY ACTIONS			
HABITAT			

ADDITIONAL NOTES

BIRD WATCHING

DATE		TIME	
LOCATION			
WEATHER		**WIND**	
BIRD NAME			
SCIENTIFIC NAME			
FEATURES/ DESCRIPTION			
BIRDS ACTIONS			
MY ACTIONS			
HABITAT			

ADDITIONAL NOTES

BIRD WATCHING

DATE		TIME	
LOCATION			
WEATHER		WIND	
BIRD NAME			
SCIENTIFIC NAME			
FEATURES/ DESCRIPTION			
BIRDS ACTIONS			
MY ACTIONS			
HABITAT			

ADDITIONAL NOTES

BIRD WATCHING

DATE		TIME	
LOCATION			
WEATHER		**WIND**	
BIRD NAME			
SCIENTIFIC NAME			
FEATURES/ DESCRIPTION			
BIRDS ACTIONS			
MY ACTIONS			
HABITAT			

ADDITIONAL NOTES

BIRD WATCHING

DATE		TIME	
LOCATION			
WEATHER		**WIND**	
BIRD NAME			
SCIENTIFIC NAME			
FEATURES/ DESCRIPTION			
BIRDS ACTIONS			
MY ACTIONS			
HABITAT			

 ADDITIONAL NOTES

BIRD WATCHING

DATE		TIME	
LOCATION			
WEATHER		**WIND**	
BIRD NAME			
SCIENTIFIC NAME			
FEATURES/ DESCRIPTION			
BIRDS ACTIONS			
MY ACTIONS			
HABITAT			

ADDITIONAL NOTES

BIRD WATCHING

DATE		TIME	
LOCATION			
WEATHER		WIND	
BIRD NAME			
SCIENTIFIC NAME			
FEATURES/ DESCRIPTION			
BIRDS ACTIONS			
MY ACTIONS			
HABITAT			

ADDITIONAL NOTES

BIRD WATCHING

DATE		TIME	
LOCATION			
WEATHER		**WIND**	
BIRD NAME			
SCIENTIFIC NAME			
FEATURES/ DESCRIPTION			
BIRDS ACTIONS			
MY ACTIONS			
HABITAT			

ADDITIONAL NOTES

BIRD WATCHING

DATE		TIME	
LOCATION			
WEATHER		**WIND**	
BIRD NAME			
SCIENTIFIC NAME			
FEATURES/ DESCRIPTION			
BIRDS ACTIONS			
MY ACTIONS			
HABITAT			

ADDITIONAL NOTES

BIRD WATCHING

DATE		TIME	
LOCATION			
WEATHER		**WIND**	
BIRD NAME			
SCIENTIFIC NAME			
FEATURES/ DESCRIPTION			
BIRDS ACTIONS			
MY ACTIONS			
HABITAT			

ADDITIONAL NOTES

BIRD WATCHING

DATE		TIME	
LOCATION			
WEATHER		**WIND**	
BIRD NAME			
SCIENTIFIC NAME			
FEATURES/ DESCRIPTION			
BIRDS ACTIONS			
MY ACTIONS			
HABITAT			

ADDITIONAL NOTES

BIRD WATCHING

DATE		TIME	
LOCATION			
WEATHER		**WIND**	
BIRD NAME			
SCIENTIFIC NAME			
FEATURES/ DESCRIPTION			
BIRDS ACTIONS			
MY ACTIONS			
HABITAT			

ADDITIONAL NOTES

BIRD WATCHING

DATE		TIME	
LOCATION			
WEATHER		**WIND**	
BIRD NAME			
SCIENTIFIC NAME			
FEATURES/ DESCRIPTION			
BIRDS ACTIONS			
MY ACTIONS			
HABITAT			

ADDITIONAL NOTES

BIRD WATCHING

DATE		TIME	
LOCATION			
WEATHER		WIND	
BIRD NAME			
SCIENTIFIC NAME			
FEATURES/ DESCRIPTION			
BIRDS ACTIONS			
MY ACTIONS			
HABITAT			

ADDITIONAL NOTES

BIRD WATCHING

DATE		TIME	
LOCATION			
WEATHER		**WIND**	
BIRD NAME			
SCIENTIFIC NAME			
FEATURES/ DESCRIPTION			
BIRDS ACTIONS			
MY ACTIONS			
HABITAT			

ADDITIONAL NOTES

BIRD WATCHING

DATE		TIME	
LOCATION			
WEATHER		**WIND**	
BIRD NAME			
SCIENTIFIC NAME			
FEATURES/ DESCRIPTION			
BIRDS ACTIONS			
MY ACTIONS			
HABITAT			

 ADDITIONAL NOTES

BIRD WATCHING

DATE		TIME	
LOCATION			
WEATHER		**WIND**	
BIRD NAME			
SCIENTIFIC NAME			
FEATURES/ DESCRIPTION			
BIRDS ACTIONS			
MY ACTIONS			
HABITAT			

ADDITIONAL NOTES

BIRD WATCHING

DATE		TIME	
LOCATION			
WEATHER		**WIND**	
BIRD NAME			
SCIENTIFIC NAME			
FEATURES/ DESCRIPTION			
BIRDS ACTIONS			
MY ACTIONS			
HABITAT			

ADDITIONAL NOTES

BIRD WATCHING

DATE		TIME	
LOCATION			
WEATHER		**WIND**	
BIRD NAME			
SCIENTIFIC NAME			
FEATURES/ DESCRIPTION			
BIRDS ACTIONS			
MY ACTIONS			
HABITAT			

ADDITIONAL NOTES

BIRD WATCHING

DATE		TIME	
LOCATION			
WEATHER		**WIND**	
BIRD NAME			
SCIENTIFIC NAME			
FEATURES/ DESCRIPTION			
BIRDS ACTIONS			
MY ACTIONS			
HABITAT			

ADDITIONAL NOTES

BIRD WATCHING

DATE		TIME	
LOCATION			
WEATHER		**WIND**	
BIRD NAME			
SCIENTIFIC NAME			
FEATURES/ DESCRIPTION			
BIRDS ACTIONS			
MY ACTIONS			
HABITAT			

 ADDITIONAL NOTES

BIRD WATCHING

DATE		TIME	
LOCATION			
WEATHER		WIND	
BIRD NAME			
SCIENTIFIC NAME			
FEATURES/ DESCRIPTION			
BIRDS ACTIONS			
MY ACTIONS			
HABITAT			

ADDITIONAL NOTES

BIRD WATCHING

DATE		TIME	
LOCATION			
WEATHER		**WIND**	
BIRD NAME			
SCIENTIFIC NAME			
FEATURES/ DESCRIPTION			
BIRDS ACTIONS			
MY ACTIONS			
HABITAT			

ADDITIONAL NOTES

BIRD WATCHING

DATE		TIME	
LOCATION			
WEATHER		**WIND**	
BIRD NAME			
SCIENTIFIC NAME			
FEATURES/ DESCRIPTION			
BIRDS ACTIONS			
MY ACTIONS			
HABITAT			

ADDITIONAL NOTES

BIRD WATCHING

DATE		TIME	
LOCATION			
WEATHER		**WIND**	
BIRD NAME			
SCIENTIFIC NAME			
FEATURES/ DESCRIPTION			
BIRDS ACTIONS			
MY ACTIONS			
HABITAT			

ADDITIONAL NOTES

BIRD WATCHING

DATE		**TIME**	
LOCATION			
WEATHER		**WIND**	
BIRD NAME			
SCIENTIFIC NAME			
FEATURES/ DESCRIPTION			
BIRDS ACTIONS			
MY ACTIONS			
HABITAT			

ADDITIONAL NOTES

BIRD WATCHING

DATE		TIME	
LOCATION			
WEATHER		WIND	
BIRD NAME			
SCIENTIFIC NAME			
FEATURES/ DESCRIPTION			
BIRDS ACTIONS			
MY ACTIONS			
HABITAT			

ADDITIONAL NOTES

BIRD WATCHING

DATE		TIME	
LOCATION			
WEATHER		WIND	
BIRD NAME			
SCIENTIFIC NAME			
FEATURES/ DESCRIPTION			
BIRDS ACTIONS			
MY ACTIONS			
HABITAT			

ADDITIONAL NOTES

BIRD WATCHING

DATE		TIME	
LOCATION			
WEATHER		**WIND**	
BIRD NAME			
SCIENTIFIC NAME			
FEATURES/ DESCRIPTION			
BIRDS ACTIONS			
MY ACTIONS			
HABITAT			

ADDITIONAL NOTES

BIRD WATCHING

DATE		TIME	
LOCATION			
WEATHER		WIND	
BIRD NAME			
SCIENTIFIC NAME			
FEATURES/ DESCRIPTION			
BIRDS ACTIONS			
MY ACTIONS			
HABITAT			

ADDITIONAL NOTES

BIRD WATCHING

DATE		TIME	
LOCATION			
WEATHER		**WIND**	
BIRD NAME			
SCIENTIFIC NAME			
FEATURES/ DESCRIPTION			
BIRDS ACTIONS			
MY ACTIONS			
HABITAT			

ADDITIONAL NOTES

BIRD WATCHING

DATE		TIME	
LOCATION			
WEATHER		**WIND**	
BIRD NAME			
SCIENTIFIC NAME			
FEATURES/ DESCRIPTION			
BIRDS ACTIONS			
MY ACTIONS			
HABITAT			

ADDITIONAL NOTES

BIRD WATCHING

DATE		TIME	
LOCATION			
WEATHER		WIND	
BIRD NAME			
SCIENTIFIC NAME			
FEATURES/ DESCRIPTION			
BIRDS ACTIONS			
MY ACTIONS			
HABITAT			

ADDITIONAL NOTES

BIRD WATCHING

DATE		TIME	
LOCATION			
WEATHER		**WIND**	
BIRD NAME			
SCIENTIFIC NAME			
FEATURES/ DESCRIPTION			
BIRDS ACTIONS			
MY ACTIONS			
HABITAT			

ADDITIONAL NOTES

BIRD WATCHING

DATE		TIME	
LOCATION			
WEATHER		WIND	
BIRD NAME			
SCIENTIFIC NAME			
FEATURES/ DESCRIPTION			
BIRDS ACTIONS			
MY ACTIONS			
HABITAT			

ADDITIONAL NOTES

BIRD WATCHING

DATE		TIME	
LOCATION			
WEATHER		**WIND**	
BIRD NAME			
SCIENTIFIC NAME			
FEATURES/ DESCRIPTION			
BIRDS ACTIONS			
MY ACTIONS			
HABITAT			

ADDITIONAL NOTES

BIRD WATCHING

DATE		TIME	
LOCATION			
WEATHER		**WIND**	
BIRD NAME			
SCIENTIFIC NAME			
FEATURES/ DESCRIPTION			
BIRDS ACTIONS			
MY ACTIONS			
HABITAT			

ADDITIONAL NOTES

BIRD WATCHING

DATE		TIME	
LOCATION			
WEATHER		**WIND**	
BIRD NAME			
SCIENTIFIC NAME			
FEATURES/ DESCRIPTION			
BIRDS ACTIONS			
MY ACTIONS			
HABITAT			

 ADDITIONAL NOTES

BIRD WATCHING

DATE		TIME	
LOCATION			
WEATHER		**WIND**	
BIRD NAME			
SCIENTIFIC NAME			
FEATURES/ DESCRIPTION			
BIRDS ACTIONS			
MY ACTIONS			
HABITAT			

ADDITIONAL NOTES

BIRD WATCHING

DATE		TIME	
LOCATION			
WEATHER		**WIND**	
BIRD NAME			
SCIENTIFIC NAME			
FEATURES/ DESCRIPTION			
BIRDS ACTIONS			
MY ACTIONS			
HABITAT			

 ADDITIONAL NOTES

BIRD WATCHING

DATE		TIME	
LOCATION			
WEATHER		**WIND**	
BIRD NAME			
SCIENTIFIC NAME			
FEATURES/ DESCRIPTION			
BIRDS ACTIONS			
MY ACTIONS			
HABITAT			

ADDITIONAL NOTES

BIRD WATCHING

DATE		TIME	
LOCATION			
WEATHER		**WIND**	
BIRD NAME			
SCIENTIFIC NAME			
FEATURES/ DESCRIPTION			
BIRDS ACTIONS			
MY ACTIONS			
HABITAT			

ADDITIONAL NOTES

BIRD WATCHING

DATE		TIME	
LOCATION			
WEATHER		**WIND**	
BIRD NAME			
SCIENTIFIC NAME			
FEATURES/ DESCRIPTION			
BIRDS ACTIONS			
MY ACTIONS			
HABITAT			

ADDITIONAL NOTES

BIRD WATCHING

DATE		TIME	
LOCATION			
WEATHER		**WIND**	
BIRD NAME			
SCIENTIFIC NAME			
FEATURES/ DESCRIPTION			
BIRDS ACTIONS			
MY ACTIONS			
HABITAT			

ADDITIONAL NOTES

BIRD WATCHING

DATE		TIME	
LOCATION			
WEATHER		**WIND**	
BIRD NAME			
SCIENTIFIC NAME			
FEATURES/ DESCRIPTION			
BIRDS ACTIONS			
MY ACTIONS			
HABITAT			

ADDITIONAL NOTES

Made in the USA
Columbia, SC
27 May 2023

17398136R00059